I0107601

TIERS OF HEALING III

Self Guided Workbook...Journey To A New Vision

by

ANNE BROWNING

Copyright © 2013 Anne Browning

All rights reserved.

ISBN: 0977150348

ISBN-13: 9780977150342

Library of Congress Control Number: 2013909150

PGS Incorporated Publishing

Sedona, AZ

TIERS OF HEALING
OVERVIEW & WELCOME

Welcome to Tiers of Healing. We have been where you are. Each of us has suffered great loss, grieved, and thought life would never be good again. Life will be good again. If we were able to move from a place of hopelessness and despair to a place where there was a glimmer of hope, we know you will be able to do the same. If we were able to build on that hope, find a grudging sense of acceptance for what we lost, we know that you will be able to do it as well. If each of us was able to find a new vision for what would one day become our new normal, we are certain it is possible for you. Finally, if we, with little support, were able to take the steps to reach that vision and live a full and joyful life, we know you will be able to take those steps. We are here to support you.

Tiers of Healing was originally designed to be facilitated in small groups. That product is still available, and there are groups that meet to move through all the Tiers of loss, finding hope and friendship along the way. What you have purchased has many of the components of our group program, but it is designed for individual study. We urge you to find someone to share your journey with, perhaps a trusted friend, mentor, or coach. We welcome your sharing through anne@tiersofhealing.com.

To make the most of this material, allow yourself the gift of time. Healing loss is possible if you decide to do the necessary work. The amount of time will vary for each individual, but a maximum of three hours a day and minimum of forty minutes is a good place to begin. Know you are not alone. The exercises in these workbooks are not difficult, yet they can be profound and must be assimilated to move forward.

Find a quiet place and consecrate it for your healing. Bless the space, perhaps adding flowers or meaningful mementos. You will need a place to write and writing materials. Some exercises ask you to have crayons or even modeling clay. Please note supplies needed at the start of each session.

A session takes approximately 10–15 minutes to read (some maybe longer) with anywhere from 15–30 minutes for the exercises.

We have included a Weather Report Chart. This is an important tool, and we urge you to copy it and keep it in a place where you can make notes daily. Often during times of loss and chaos, we feel as if are making no progress. The Weather Report is an excellent tool to note those days that were sunny and aid you in noting what you did or what you were thinking that helped make the sunny day. Equally, it can be a great way to note if you are in a place where day after day, week after week you appear to be getting worse. We urge each of you to care for yourself and to seek professional help in addition to this self-help guide. It may take a village to raise a child, but it takes an army to heal a loss.

We celebrate your courage. Loss must be healed. It has a way of hiding deep within the soul robbing us of energy, joy, and motivation. We believe we have "gotten past it," yet as we view the world, we are easily angered, tire more quickly, or just see the world as a place of dreary sameness. Once the hurt is healed, the joy in living returns, and life once again becomes hopeful.

At no time do we tell you it is not painful. It is. At no time do we tell you that you will stop the missing. You won't. At no time do we tell you that life will be like it used to be. It will not. What we will tell you is that pain comes to us all, but misery is a choice and you can choose out of it. We will tell you there is always something to miss as you grow, yet there can be smiles, laughter, and joyful memories, not longing. Finally we will tell you that you do not know what is up ahead. Life has changed, and there will be more joys, more laughter, more love, and it will be different than it was. It will be your new normal, and you may like it. There is at least hope that you will one day be on the other side of your loss, and you will be okay. We know; we have travelled the path and we are okay. Most days we are better than okay.

Welcome, we are here for you and with you.

Contact info:
anne@tiersofhealing.com

ACKNOWLEDGMENTS

Tiers of Healing Self-Study Guides are based on a program Linda Debelser Owen and I created, that is designed for small groups. Tiers of Healing for groups, was and continues to be a mission of love for both myself and Linda. I owe a deep thanks to Linda for her vision, her dedication, and most importantly, her friendship.

There were months and months of talks, writing, rewriting, editing and editing and rewriting. Not once did I hear Linda complain about the work involved. She kept her eye on her vision of reaching hurting people and helping them heal. Linda lives in Canada and runs the Canadian Tiers program. She has delivered the group material to churches, women fighting breast cancer, indigenous people who are still recovering from land loss and she is the woman I turn to when I need a laugh, a push or a strong shoulder. She is my hero. I acknowledge her expertise, her commitment, her integrity and her love.

I want to acknowledge all the men, women and children who have had a loss and continue to live their lives fully and who have the compassion to reach out to others who are in pain. I acknowledge those to whom this book is dedicated, individuals who are in pain and feel alone. I assure you, you are *not* alone.

We are here and we have known your pain.

Donna Lipman of Austin Texas is the woman who recorded the DVD portion of the Tiers of Healing for Groups. She is a woman of deep compassion, brilliant insights. Her commitment to filling our world with peace and joy was begun at birth. Everyone adores Donna. She has delivered the Tiers for Groups in Austin and she used the material in a very real way when her husband, Terry Lipman, who did the filming for the DVD, died suddenly. I acknowledge her, love her and treasure her friendship.

My husband, Peter Schroeder, helped Linda and I with the editing and reading of Tiers of Healing for Groups. He was instrumental in getting the Tiers of Healing Self Study Guides completed and is editing Tiers of Helping and Tiers of Hope. Peter is the miracle that God sent to me as answered prayer in 1988. He continues to inspire me, strengthen me, hold me and without him my life would be much less bright. I love you, Peter.

Finally, I must acknowledge my mentor, teacher and friend, Debbie Ford. Thank you, Debbie for your work, your guidance, your love.

TIERS OF HEALING
Tier III: Journey to a New Vision

CONTENTS

TIERS OF HEALING III
SESSION 1
SELF-CARE REVIEW

Acceptance of ourselves is the beginning of personal growth and transformation. In accepting ourselves, we face the fact of our own fragility and incompleteness, and it is by acknowledging that we are incomplete that we can change. Peace of mind is achieved not by filling in the gaps or correcting the flaws in our personality, but in understanding these flaws and accepting them as part of our reality.
From *Gardening the Soul* by Sister Stanislaus Kennedy

Music: "Welcome to Wherever You Are" by Bon Jovi

In Tier II we talked about acceptance and moving you to the next stage of healing. This is what Tier III is all about. As we begin our journey to a new vision for our lives, it is important for us to acknowledge where we are now. We ended Tier II by honoring ourselves at the deepest level. Please be certain you continue with this important task. You may want to add a time to honor yourself on your Self-Care Contract.

Please continue tracking your moods and emotions. You may compare these emotions to the weather (i.e., sad=rainy; happy=sunny; angry=stormy). What is important is that you keep a record of your progress. At times loss can be so overwhelming that it is easy to lose track of what strides we make.

Remember that it is your responsibility to put yourself first, to love yourself unconditionally, and to nurture yourself when you need nurturing. When you take care of yourself first, you then become able to take care of others.

At the end of Tier I, we asked you to get an acknowledgment box, and at the end of Tier II, we asked that you continue to use it and begin the practice of honoring yourself at the deepest level. We ask you to continue both practices. We also talked about gratitude and had you make a list of all the things to be grateful for in various areas of your life. We urge you to continue setting aside time to dwell on what you are grateful for. Gratitude is your doorway to joy.

We have many fun activities in this Tier as you begin to explore your new vision for your life.

Please fill out your Self-Care Contract now. Place it where you will be able to review it daily. Additional self-care is to be added as you become stronger. In the early stages of grief, just getting out of bed or brushing your teeth may have been all the self-care you were able to achieve. By this time you will have your acknowledgment box, a time to honor all you are and all you have done, and a time to list what you are grateful for. It may be a great time to include times for visiting friends, time for laughter, better nutrition, or an exercise plan. Push yourself a small amount as you complete your Contract.

Remember, we are here. We are your number one cheerleaders!

SELF – CARE CONTRACT

I, _____, commit myself to the following self-care beginning this week. (List what you will actually do.)

_____

_____

_____

_____

_____

_____

_____

_____

_____

(Make sure this is a realistic and measurable plan.)

I will begin working on self-care _____ for _____

                                       DATE   **LENGTH OF TIME**

When I achieve this goal, I will reward myself with:

I will evaluate the achievement of this goal with my support person. (Be certain to find someone to hold you accountable for this contract.)

Name: _____

Date: _____

Contacted by: _____ (how will you contact your "buddy"?

phone, e-mail, in person)

Signed: _____

Support: _____ Date: _____

Exercises for Session 1

1. Continue to use a place for your "inner work," a place to listen to or read uplifting words. Be sure it is a place you enjoy and take pride in. This could be a separate room, a corner in a closet, or a special chair that you feel safe in and bless it with your thoughts. This is a sacred place, so treasure it.

2. Take five minutes daily to be in this special place and say the words, "Today I will remember to honor myself at the deepest level. Today I will remember I am not alone."

3. With this Tier, we ask that you begin to track your ideas of what you may have wanted to do as a young child ("What do you want to be when you grow up?"). Track your dreams of a possible future, what your heart longs to do or be. Do not judge this list. It is only for you, and you may write whatever you want. We suggest you leave this list somewhere you can easily add to it (a bathroom counter is a great place) as you think of what you have always wanted to do, to be, to explore, or to create. Allow your spirit to take over.

Weather Report Chart
Month/Year

Sun	Mon	Tues	Wed	Thu	Fri	Sat

Weather Report Chart
Month/Year (Continued)

Sun	Mon	Tues	Wed	Thu	Fri	Sat

TIERS OF HEALING III
SESSION 2
THOUGHT

Without uncertainty and the unknown, life is just the stale repetition of outworn memories. You become the victim of the past, and your tormentor today is yourself left over from yesterday.
Deepak Chopra from *The Seven Spiritual Laws of Success*

Song: "Our Thoughts Are Prayers" by Lesley Ann Smith

At no other time in history is there so much to assimilate concerning the power of thought. *The Secret*, a movie we would recommend you watch, became a huge phenomenon with little or no advertising. Deepak Chopra, a leader in the scientific accumulation of evidence regarding the dynamic nature of thought, is a respected physician who has taken the idea of choosing our thoughts and created numerous best-selling books. Industry is employing vision boards and realizing the importance of meditation to assure creativity. If you were to Google the word *thought*, you would find 585,000,000 results.

Your thoughts are powerful. Before you go much further with your reading, try this exercise:

1. Stand with your arms by your side and turn as far to the right as you are able to turn. Note what you are able to see, how far you are able to turn.

2. Now repeat this on your left.

3. Now stand with your arms by your side and <u>your eyes closed,</u> and ***imagine*** turning to the right. Continue ***imagining*** that you are turning completely around, as if you were able to turn on an axis and look behind you completely. ***Now imagine that instead of turning back to the front your body was able to twist itself all the way around to the front!*** Allow yourself to imagine this fully, what it may feel like, what you would be able to do with this amazing ability, and now ***imagine*** your body spinning back to the front.

4. Now, turn to the right and notice how much farther you were able to turn. Some people who have done this exercise are able to turn 50 percent more! Even if you were only able to turn to the right 5 percent more, you will notice your thoughts and your ***imagination*** assisted you in achieving better results. What could you do if you were able to feel 5–50 percent better? What could you accomplish with 5–50 percent more creative abilities? If you were able to accumulate 5–50 percent more money, would that be a blessing? It is possible. You only need practice.

5. Now, allow yourself to practice on your left side. What did you notice?

Thoughts can be utilized to assist you in creating what will one day become your "new normal." Your thoughts create your reality; you may choose what those thoughts will be, or you may allow thoughts to just "pop" up in your mind and control you and the life that is yours to live.

Are you interested in changing your thoughts? Are you aware of what thoughts play inside of your brain, looping over and over again, a litany that sometimes seems impossible to turn off? The first fact to be aware of as you tackle your thoughts is that it is impossible to have more than one thought broadcasting at any given time. You may feel as if this is not true because thoughts come so quickly, but the good news is that one thought at a time is the reality. This is great news because if you have a thought that disempowers, sabotages, or takes you into pain, you can put a different one in its place.

It sounds easy—just change your thoughts and you change your life. It is simple, but it is far from easy. Change and transformation takes focus and awareness. Your first step is to become aware of what your thoughts are. Notice if many of your thoughts begin with the word "should" (I should be better by now; I should box up the old clothes; I should stop eating so much. The list of "shoulds" is endless). Play a game with yourself and replace "should" with "could." Catch yourself and notice the difference in how you feel about yourself.

Do you find that your thoughts take on an "if only" thread? Perhaps it may sound something like this: "If only he hadn't left, I could stop working." "If only she had gone to the doctor sooner, she would be here now." "If only I was older, younger, thinner, fatter, taller, shorter, then life would be better." It is normal to have the "if onlies"; however know that these types of thoughts get you nowhere. What the "if onlies" do get you is depression, frustration, regret, and a sense of hopelessness. These are not feelings that will assist you on the way to what is to become your new normal, the life that is waiting for you to step into it. "If onlies" provide no forward action. Forward action will move you into a place where you can leave victimization and stand courageously in a place of hope.

When the "if onlies" come (and they will), replace them with the "what can I dos to better." Consider the following examples: "What can I do at sixty-five years of age that will better my life?" "Now that she is gone, what can I do to better my life right now?" "He left a year ago, so what can I do to feel better about myself?" Yes, these are tricks, but they work. Loss takes time to heal, and a new way to live takes time to develop. Use your thoughts to bolster and encourage yourself. Eventually you will have created that new normal and have come through loss without getting trapped somewhere in the middle.

Thoughts are powerful vehicles to shape our future. In the suggested song, "Our Thoughts Are Prayers," there is a line that states, "our thoughts are prayers and we are always praying." What type of future are you praying for? Do you call out to God to give you a new spouse, a better job, better health, and then allow thoughts of being alone in your old age, going on Welfare, or dying before you have had a chance to enter your awareness? Guard your thoughts. Align your thoughts, and be conscious of them.

The way to begin to change your disempowering thoughts is to become aware of your thoughts first. As Dr. Phil says, "You cannot change what you don't acknowledge." Once you are able to recognize your disempowering thoughts, you can begin to flex the muscle of positive thinking. Each time you flex the muscle of positive thought, you strengthen that muscle. You begin to form a habit of positive thinking. Our habits make us. Change your habits and change yourself.

Whatever you plant in your subconscious mind and nourish every day with conviction and emotion will one day become a reality. Constant repetition will result in a change in your behavior. What you think you will become. We know this through personal experience. We invite you to Google this theory and read the multitude of books and articles dating back hundreds of years that propose the power we each have been given.

We attract and create our own limitations with our thoughts. Our thoughts turn into beliefs, and our beliefs manifest our results. Because we are powerful enough to attract and create our limitations, it also means we are powerful enough to break through them. Do not allow your thoughts to limit you. Use them to empower yourself.

What if you have no real idea which thoughts take up space? What if you try to think positive thoughts and you still seem to sabotage yourself? An excellent book that addresses the power of our hidden beliefs and thoughts is *The Secret of the Shadow.* Number one best-selling author, Debbie Ford, writes about how our beliefs may be formed from thoughts we had when very young. Any of her books will assist people wishing to transform their lives, and her trained and certified coaches are able to guide individuals to find and reframe old worn-out thoughts and beliefs.

Of all the incredible truths we've learned about the soul, none is more empowering than this: **You are the master of your own thoughts and the creator of your reality**. Positive thoughts and actions can never generate negative results, just as negative thoughts and actions can never bring forth positive results. We all understand this in the natural world. We all know that flower seeds will only produce flowers while weeds will only produce more weeds. We need to understand that our minds work the same way.

Suffering is always the result of a negative or disempowering thought process. It's a sign that you are out of harmony with yourself. Your thoughts may have been directed toward what you do not have rather than what you do. Be very clear that suffering is not pain and pain is not suffering. All humans, if they live long enough, will experience pain. Our goal, and we hope yours as well, is to limit suffering. Loss is painful. There is grief, then the challenge of accepting what seems unacceptable, and then rebuilding a life that no longer has what we once had. Use your thoughts to remind yourself that you have no idea how your life may be used or what good lies in the future. The truth is, no one knows what lies ahead. Decide now to use your thoughts and your imagination to set up a future that is free of suffering, a life filled with satisfaction and meaning. What does that look like to you?

Our thoughts can set us up for failure or be our greatest source of encouragement. It is up to us to point them in the direction that is most supportive of us. Our thoughts are the key to our emotional, physical, and spiritual well-being. Our thoughts and the way we think of ourselves are the only things that can bring about the changes we crave in our lives.

God gave us free will. It is up to us to use free will the way He intended. The purpose of free will is to produce love and joy for ourselves; this enables us to give love and joy to others, which in turn attracts love and joy to us from those we love, those around us, and the universe as a whole. What we think is what we will attract into our lives.

What are *you* thinking?

Exercises Session 2

1. On a sheet of paper, make five columns. In the first will be a list of all the thoughts that limit you. Now in the next column, write down where that thought came from (a parent, teacher, sibling, you made it up, etc.). The third column will hold how long that thought has limited you (since second grade math class, since your divorce, how long?). The fourth notes if this is a daily, weekly, or occasional thought. Finally in the last column, write if you would like to keep this thought and for how much longer (Yes, for at least another month.). You can add to this list on a continual basis as you become more and more aware of your thoughts.

2. On a separate sheet of paper, create two columns. The first will again hold the limiting, worn-out thought and the second the new more empowering thought. Again, you may add to this list at any time, and if you decide you no longer want the new thought and would like to take the old thought back, you may do that. They are *your thoughts, and it is up to you to decide what you want.*

3. Challenge yourself, and as you say what used to be true, stop and say out loud that this was how you *were.* Change is constant. Perhaps you thought you did not like parties—that can change. Perhaps you were afraid to speak up for yourself—that can change. Maybe you were sad for a long time—that can change. What would it feel like to say, "I used to be alone, but that is changing," "I used to be afraid to sing in public, but that is changing," "I was intimidated by men, but that is changing"? Try on the words; try on the thoughts and notice how you feel.

TIERS OF HEALING III
SESSION 3
RECEIVING

Let the universe help you. You are not alone. You never have been, although your belief may have created that illusion.
Melody Beattie in *Journey to the Heart*

Song: "Receiving Love" by Kathy Lowe

In the previous session, you read about the power of thought and how we can become aware of and change our thoughts. In this session we will continue that practice with learning to receive. Learning to receive for many of us will mean changing our thoughts. All of us have heard that it is more blessed to give than to receive. Take a moment and read the following sentence out loud: "I must receive if I am to give."

Take a moment and reflect on what is a direct order from flight attendants: "Before helping another with an oxygen mask, apply your mask." Now ask yourself, "Why is it important to secure ourselves before we can give to others?"

We are only able to give to the extent that we are able to receive. If we are unable or unwilling to receive from others or God or the Universe, we will soon become depleted and will be of no use to ourselves or others. We are designed to receive. A newborn must first breathe *in* before the miracle of breathing in and out begins.

During times of extreme change, it is vital that we care for ourselves daily. It is vital that we ask for and receive that which will help us on our journey.

Is it a hug that you need most? A time with a friend doing nothing more than eating popcorn and laughing in the movies, or someone to help make sense of your end-of-year statement—what do you most need right now?

Humans love to help when there is a direct need. Whenever there is a fundraiser, natural catastrophe, blood drive, or something as simple as a bake sale, people step up. They give so others may receive.

A wonderful movie is *Pay It Forward* in which a young boy begins a movement in which people begin to help with no intention of getting anything in return, but the person receiving agrees to pass on the kindness in whatever way is presented. If you truly have trouble receiving, make a pact with yourself to "Pay It Forward."

In Debbie Ford's work with shadow beliefs, she has identified a few key beliefs human beings carry deep in their hearts. Common beliefs that thousands, perhaps millions of people share are: "I am not worthy" and "I am not good enough." These beliefs are deep within the unconscious, and many have no idea they have such a debilitating belief. On a conscious level, they may profess to have great self-esteem or self-worth, yet these same people find it difficult to ask for help or accept compliments, offers of assistance, or even gifts. If you would like to explore this issue in depth, please read Ms. Ford's book, *Secret of the Shadow*. Once you are able to see yourself as worthy, accept that you are in fact good enough, it may be possible to receive all that the Universe has to give you today and in the future.

Exercise Session 3

1. You will need white paper and crayons and perhaps magazines or old photos.

2. Set aside one hour with soft and gentle music playing during the exercise.

3. Allow yourself to receive an answer to the question, "What keeps me from truly receiving?"

4. You may look through your old photos or pictures in magazines to help spark an answer, or you may just begin to draw with your crayons on the white paper what you believe keeps you from receiving all that is available to you. Is it doubt? Fear? Your family's voice that you are selfish? The feeling of being in someone's debt? Allow yourself to hear, see, and sense all the reasons you may have trouble receiving now and in the past.

5. Draw what blocks you. If it is doubt, imagine what doubt may look like and draw that. If it is fear, what does fear look like? What color is it, and how big? Just use your imagination and draw. No one need see it, and absolutely no person will judge your drawing. If you judge it, stop it.

6. Begin to keep a "what I received today" journal or chart. Just note all that is given to you and all the ways you are helped. Notice your gratitude growing.

TIERS OF HEALING III
SESSION 4
INTENT

Intent is what makes him invulnerable. Intent is what sends a shaman through a wall, through space, to infinity.
—Carlos Castaneda

Song: "High Hopes" by J. Van Heusen/S. Cahn

The dictionary has four definitions given for the word **intent:**

in·tent

[1] [in-**tent**]

noun

1. something that is <u>intended</u>; purpose; design; <u>intention</u>: *The original intent of the committee was to raise funds.*
2. the act or fact of <u>intending</u>, as to do something: *criminal intent.*
3. *Law.* The state of a person's mind that directs his or her actions toward a specific <u>object</u>.
4. meaning or significance.

Thoughts are powerful, and directed thoughts are very powerful. Having an intent for our thoughts, actions, and lives creates a direction, a focus, a meaning that has the potential to assist not only us but all of humanity.

What is your intent? What do you intend to do going forward? What have you decided concerning your future? Make no mistake, if you decide your future will be dismal or if you decide your future will one day be meaningful and happy, you will be right. This is not a magic formula, and it takes a great deal of work and perseverance. Yet bookshelves are filled with stories of individuals who allowed themselves a specific intent and then held onto that intent for dear life. This is not a modern idea or some type of psychobabble.

Intent is mentioned in the Bible. "**As a man thinketh, so** is he," Proverbs 23:7. Intent is the basis for the best-selling film, *The Secret,* and Winston Churchill used intent to inspire the free world during the dark days of World War II.

If intent is so powerful, why do so few people utilize its strength? The answer is as simple as it is complicated. Intent takes focus; it takes change; it takes work! Notice as you read these words the thoughts that run through your mind. You may be agreeing with what you are reading or having doubts, and at the same time, your brain is feeding you random unconnected thoughts. "What will I have for dinner?" "My leg is falling asleep." "Did I leave the stove on?" Our thoughts seem to come to us unbidden and uncontrolled. No one has told us we can choose. We can change. We have the power to choose. We can decide to have intent and hold intentional thoughts.

What does it look like to "have intent"? Simply put it is making a conscious decision to have thoughts that support what you want to be, what you want to have, or what you want to do. Intent is remaining conscious of where you are going.

Imagine for a moment waking up at the airport. You have no recollection of how you got there or where you came from; all you know is that there are planes everywhere going to thousands of destinations. You may feel afraid. The noise and confusion seem overwhelming. People approach asking you where you are going and what you are doing, but you have no earthly idea. You have a credit card in your wallet and photos of a beautiful setting with mountains and a brilliant blue lake. The mountains are snowcapped, and sailboats are on the lake. You decide that is where you want to go. You want to step into that photo and feel the peace and tranquility it seems to offer.

Now imagine that what you do next is get in a line that sells tickets, and as you approach the ticket agent, he asks where you want to go. You pull out the photo and point. There is a line of people behind you with tickets and luggage, and the ticket agent gives you a hard look that says, "Get out of my line." You to step out of line, quickly.

Still at the airport, you begin to wander from line to line. The smell of coffee lures you into a Starbucks, and for the time being, you forget about mountain lakes. Now you notice a bookstore, which you enter and buy a paperback by your favorite author. You realize that you have been at the airport for four hours, and it is getting dark outside. You notice a sign for an airport hotel and check in.

The desk clerk wants to know if you would like a wake-up call and if you have an early flight. Notice how much time you have spent going nowhere. This is a far-fetched example of what so many individuals do on a daily basis. Is this what you want to do?

Many, many, many individuals get up every morning to an alarm clock set for a time that will allow just enough time to grab a coffee and get to work or school. They have no intent for the day, week, month, or year. Perhaps they hold an intention of what they hope to do on the weekend but, if asked, would respond that their boss controls their time and their kids control their schedule. Seventy percent of individuals when polled responded that they did not like their jobs. The day of the week in which most deaths occur is Monday. What if an intent was made on Sunday that a person's week would be filled with laughter? Do you think it may change a person's satisfaction level? A person's health? A person's longevity?

The setting of an intent is simple. Decide what you want to feel today, or what you want to do, who you want to be. It *must be somewhat realistic.* You may want to loose fifteen pounds by this evening, but that will most likely not happen. But it is possible to set an intent to avoid sugar today. You could set the intent to drink eight glasses of water today or be conscious as you eat. Set your intent, and better yet, write it down and carry it with you.

Humans are creatures of habit, and your car will pull into the drive-through at Starbucks. You will want to say, "I'll have a venti mocha, whipped cream, and an apple fritter." Keep your intent. Hold it as you catch yourself and say, "I will have a small coffee black and an oatmeal." Now, watch your thoughts. "Just this once will not hurt. You can start later. You need the sugar to get going this morning. You deserve something good—you worked out for an hour this morning." It is as if you have no control over these thoughts, and they are powerful. Hold on to your intent. Imagine shutting the door on the thoughts that do not support your intent, much like you would close the door on a pesky door-to-door solicitor you did not want to hear. Be conscious. In the beginning it is much harder, and with each new intent, you must have a plan for the unhelpful thoughts. But once you realize you can have control over your thoughts, your life will begin to change.

Try having the intent to laugh daily. You will be amazed at what shows up to bring forth laughter. Play with the idea of intent and have the intent that you will be provided with good surprises during your workweek. You will then become aware of all that is good in your life.

Intent is lasered thought and, like a laser, is powerful beyond measure.

Exercise Session 4

1. Make a promise to yourself that you will play with the idea of intent. Begin with small intentions, eating five servings of fruits and veggies, smiling at one person every hour, using the word *could* in place of *should*. Write it down and carry it with you. Notice the results.

2. Now up your game. Ask your Higher Self, God, or the Universe for a weekly intent. What would be in your best interest? Be quiet for a few deep breaths and then write down what this intent is. Carry it with you. Notice the results.

3. Go the bookstore and have the intent that you will find a book that explores intent on a deeper level or you will find a DVD such as *The Secret* that explores the many ways intent can assist you and the world.

4. Notice if you have the intent to believe in the power of your intentions or if you have the intent to have little faith in what you think or choose.

TIERS OF HEALING III
SESSION 5
VISION

So you see!
There's no end to the things
You might know—
Depending how far
Beyond Zebra you go.
Dr. Seuss

Song: "One Vision One World" by DJ Bobo

What is your vision? Do you have a vision? What is a vision? Why have a vision?

During times of struggle, of change, during times of loss and rebuilding, a vision can become your best friend. A vision points the way to where you want to go. It can be the place you go to when your todays are filled with stress and your nights are long and lonely. Your vision acts as a beacon pulling you forward, helping you get out of bed in the morning. Your vision is what is waiting for you on the other side of struggle.

A vision is not a plan, nor is it a goal. A goal needs a plan, and for a vision to become a reality, it will need a goal. But without a vision, it is difficult to follow a plan or create a goal. Visions are the possibilities waiting to be born. They lie dormant waiting for you to discover them, to see them, to embrace and give them substance.

Visions can be specific, and often times they are filmy as if seen from a great distance. They are more feeling, a sense of something; sometimes they do not seem real. A vision is that small voice that says, "You could do that. I wonder what would happen if I...? What if...?"

Visions can spring from a deep longing or a passionate belief. Visions that elevate, improve, change, or shake up the status quo have moved our world forward and given us lofty ideals and a better life. Letting go of those visions moves our world into darkness. Power comes from vision.

A vision gives us a place to go, a beacon that can keep us on our path.

Is it possible to have a vision that destroys? Of course. Humanity has proven our freedom of choice, and it is up to each of us to claim our own light and in that light, find what our vision is. It is recommended that as you begin to vision you pray first. You ask to see or feel the highest for all concerned.

After working with perhaps thousands of people, we have noticed that few individuals have a vision. Often they tell us about dreams they had as children that did not materialize, and they speak of their great disappointment. Do you fear allowing a vision to take shape because you are afraid you will not get to what is waiting for you? It is vital to hold the vision. Success is truly a matter of perseverance and determination. The Universe would not put a deep longing in your heart and soul without the path to achieve it.

How do you find your vision? Visions require quiet and time alone. Native cultures knew this as they sent their young men out into the wilderness on vision quests. Facing their fears, the young men would return with a sense of purpose, direction, and confidence.

Are you ready to enter the wilderness of your soul, your spirit, your heart? Step one, want to find a vision—have the desire to find *your* vision. Step two, ask. You can literally say, out loud, "What is my vision?" or get a pad of paper and write this question at the top of a fresh page, "What is my vision?" Step three, expect an answer, asking and then assuming there will be blocks keeping the answer from coming forth. Step four, pay attention. Some people get an immediate answer in full living color and sound, but much more often hints are dropped. It is your job to begin to gather the hints. Did you hear a song that gave you an idea? Did your friend mention an article he read that quickened your heart? Maybe as you were flipping through a magazine, you saw a picture of a place that said, "this is it."

As you gather the hints, it is helpful to keep them in one location. A yellow legal pad makes an excellent place to jot ideas, thoughts, insights, or use the notepad on your smart phone. Consider and treat these hints as the treasures they are.

Step five, find a place with little or no distraction; you will bring plain white paper, crayons, and a pen with you. The place needs to be free of outside noise and responsibilities. This may require removing yourself from your daily schedule and taking a morning or afternoon to spend time in solitude. If your budget allows, find a retreat center or class that offers vision classes or sponsors vision quests. See www.tiersofhealing.com for resources and teachers. If a getaway is not possible, find solitude at a local church, synagogue, or library. Once you have found your place of solitude, allow yourself to settle into the stillness and quiet of your breathing. You may want to allow your eyes to close. Say a prayer and surround yourself with God's light or your higher power, or even imagine a beautiful bubble of wisdom and you are sitting in middle of this bubble. You are serene, still, and quiet. Breathe and feel what is there. Keep putting your attention on your breath as you feel your body relax; feel a deepening and perhaps a sense of awe or expectation. You need do nothing but breathe and wait. Now ask, "What is the vision that is waiting for me to step into?" Breathe again as you wait for an answer. Many people expect to actually see something, and some do. More often those we have worked with get a sense of something. Pay attention to what you are sensing and the feelings that surround this new sense. What does it feel like to step into this new place? Do you notice any other people in this place that waits for you? If what you are seeing is in black and white, allow yourself to be shown what it is like in color. If it is a still photo, allow movement and life to enter this vision. Do you hear words, thoughts, directions? Continue to breathe, and allow yourself to step into this place that has been waiting. Use your breath to make it real. Once you can feel the emotions surrounding this place that waits, tap your left wrist and open your eyes. Take a moment and either draw what you saw and felt or make a few notes on what your vision is.

Step six, revisit this vision again and again. Feel the feelings; experience the emotions. Believe.

Exercise Session 5

1. Make a vision board. This can be something as simple as drawing your vision in color on white paper or as involved as making a collage on poster board. What you do and how you do it is not important. What is important is that you create an outward symbol of that which you received during your visioning process. Put this vision board somewhere you will look at it daily. The front of the refrigerator is not the best place. Somewhere private where you can be with it daily is better. Take fifteen to thirty seconds **every single day** to step into your vision. Allow it to be as real as possible. Imagine seeing, hearing, smelling, touching all that is waiting for you. **Do this at least once every single day.**

2. If you want, put a date on your vision once you get a sense of when you will be ready to step into it. If you are having trouble with any of these steps, find someone to assist you or get a book about visioning. We at Tiers of Healing are always available.

TIERS OF HEALING III
SESSION 6
GOALS

I am not afraid...I was born to do this.
Joan of Arc
*Nothing can add more power to your life than concentrating all
your energies on a limited set of targets.*
Nido Qubein

Song: "Chariots of Fire" by Vangelis

Congratulations! You have reached goal setting. You have taken a look at your thoughts, focused your intent, allowed yourself to receive, and found your vision. Now it is time to create the goals that will move you toward your vision and allow your vision to become reality.

We have found that using the SMART method of goal setting and creation is possibly the most effective and time efficient practice. It is not the only way to set goals; there are hundreds of articles and books that assist people in setting goals. If you do not like this particular model, find one that speaks to you and use that. What is important is that you set goals, write your goals down, and then take the action needed to accomplish what you have written.

The acronym **SMART** stands for the specific steps in goal creation. As you use this model (or the model you choose), it is important to know why set these goals and where will they take you.

You may use goal setting for everything in your life. As you work through this session, we ask that you use the vision you found in the last session as the place you are going.

Imagine you were going on a trip—let's say to Tahiti. Tahiti would be your vision. You would have travel pamphlets about Tahiti, and you would have photos or a book about Tahiti that you had read or looked through. You would allow yourself to imagine being in Tahiti and enjoying all that you believe is waiting for you in this paradise. How to get to Tahiti would be your goal. For such a big vision, you may need several small goals: get a passport, find lodgings, obtain transportation, set up a travel budget, etc. You would probably enlist other people to help you: a travel agent, friends who have been to Tahiti, a house sitter for the time you will be gone. The list could be quite long, but your excitement about what you imagine Tahiti to be like fires your steps and gives you momentum when the list seems longer than your days. Remember, it is important to step into your vision **every day**. This will keep you on track and nourish you when the going seems too rough and too long to continue.

SMART stands for the following:

S—Specific. Make sure you are specific about your goals. That means knowing exactly what action you are going to take. What do you want to achieve? Example: Notice the difference between "I want to exercise more" and "I want to walk for thirty minutes, four times per week."

M—Measurable. Your goal must be measurable. This is the "how" part. For instance, if your goal is to lose weight, your measure might be losing two pounds per week. You'll certainly be able to see here just by stepping on the scale whether or not you have had results.

A—Achievable (on their own). This means it must be within your control and that you are not relying on someone else to help you meet the goal. Your goal should be challenging enough to make you stretch and grow.

R—Realistic. This means exactly what it says. This is where "why" comes in. Is my goal realistic? Why is it important to me? How does it fit into the bigger picture of my life?

T—Time specific. You must set a time or completion date for your goal. An end date is essential to create the urgency and momentum required to move you forward. Without a time limitation, it is easy to bump your goals onto the back burner and put them into a "someday" file. We all lead busy lives, so it becomes easy to fill our time with other things unless we specifically make time for the things that are important to us. By clearly defining the *when* of your goals, you have a guidepost to keep moving toward. Be realistic with your time constraints. Give yourself a comfortable time period in which to achieve the results you are looking for without adding too much pressure or stress to yourself and without postponing too long.

Once you have defined your goals, create a practical road map that you can follow. Without your road map, it will be easy to become lost. If you are uncertain, enlist the help of a trusted friend, mentor, or coach. That person can be your GPS system.

Accountability is vital. Who will hold you accountable for these excellent goals you have set? Set up a system to assure success. You have now invested time and energy into your intent, your vision, and now your goals. Stay committed and stay with where you know you want to be. Get an accountability partner. This person cannot be your best friend who will listen to all the reasons you did not do what you promised yourself you would accomplish this week and give you a pass. Find a friend who loves enough to confront you (in a loving way) and ask you what you could have done differently to assure completion of the task at hand. All successful people have someone that holds them accountable. Assure your success—get accountability.

Exercise Session 6

This a quick true and false quiz. See if you know what is a goal and what is not.

1. My goal is to be happy.
2. My goal is to loose seven pounds this month.
3. My goal is to be married to my high school sweetheart by next year.
4. My goal is to feel peaceful when I am with my mother.
5. My goal is to dance on Broadway.

Answers:

1. False. There is no time limit, but most importantly it is not measurable. How would five people observing you know if you were happy? How could they agree you reached your goal? A better goal, "My goal is to sing a happy song every morning for a month." You set this goal because you know when you sing a happy song you are happy.
2. True. It meets all the criteria of SMART.
3. False. This may not be realistic if the high school sweetheart does not want to get married. If the person is engaged, this then becomes a true goal.
4. False. Again, it is not measurable. See number 1.
5. False. This is not measurable and may be unrealistic if the person is fifty-year-old couch potato who has never had a dance lesson. This is actually a great vision but not a goal.

Second Exercise

Get your vision and a calendar. Imagine that you can step into your vision within a year. Set a nine-month goal, where do you need to be, what do you need to have accomplished within nine months to assure success. Now back up and set a six-month goal. What do you need to accomplish by six months that will assist you in accomplishing your six-month goal? Do the same for three months and one month. Now ask yourself what you must do this week to assure you meet your one-month goal. This will take you to your three-month goal, which will take you to your nine-month goal, which will take you to your vision. Put this on a calendar that is made of a material you can put on a wall. Put it somewhere you can see it, not inside your computer or smart phone. Once you have done this, find an accountability partner. You can post your goals on the Tiers blog at www.tiersofhealing.com.

TIERS OF HEALING III
SESSION 7
LETTING GO

*"The difference between stumbling
blocks and stepping stones is how you use them"*
Unknown Source

Song: "I Will Survive," written by Dino Fekaris, Lori Kennedy,
Frederick J. Perren, performed by Gloria Gaynor

Humans resist change, and humans who have experienced significant loss rebel when asked to change even more. Yet change is a part of life. That which does not change stagnates and eventually dies.

Observe the world we live in: day/night, seasons, tides, weather patterns, wind patterns, birth/death. The very earth we walk on, build on, shifts, changes, and moves. The caterpillar does not argue, resist, or rebel as it begins the task of spinning, changing, and transforming. Snakes go with the program of shedding skin and becoming vulnerable during the process. Birds and ducks do not ignore the call to move to a different place every winter and spring. Not one of them stays put and holds onto what he likes about his existing pond. Only humans resist change, resist letting go.

There is a quote in the Bible from Mathew 9:17 about not putting new wine in old wine skins. In biblical days wine was stored in leather wineskins instead of the bottles we currently use. New wine required new leather as old leather (old wineskins) lost the elasticity needed for the effervescence of the new wine. If a person ignored this and decided to pour new wine into the old wineskins, he or she took the chance of loosing the wine as the old wineskins could and usually did burst.

As you move toward your vision using your thoughts, your focused intent, and your well thought out goals, what old wineskins will not allow the new to be utilized? What could and does get in your way?

What beliefs, thoughts, and actions keep you from having all that you want in your life? What excuses do you use to keep yourself from having the life you long for?

Look at the emotions that stop you. Is it fear, guilt, shame, and unworthiness that keeps you tethered to powerlessness? What holds you back? Who holds you back? What are the thoughts you hear and pay attention to that would be best boxed up, put on a shelf, and not opened for at least a year? Make a list of what you believe holds you back.

Often when there has been a significant loss, one fears that what was lost will also be forgotten and the time, energy, and love will be for nothing. Love is never lost. It always remains. The shape, flavor, and texture may change and take on different colors, but the love remains. The time and energy were not wasted. They brought you to this place, and it is now time to find what your new normal will be. The fact is that you will never feel as you once did about what has been lost and you will never have that feeling you used to call normal. What you will have is a new normal, and it can be just as good, just as fulfilling, just as beautiful, but it will be different.

Humans have a great capacity to make excuses and an even greater capacity to believe the excuses are real and just. An excuse is just that, an excuse. Here are a few of the definitions from the dictionary:

3. to serve as an apology or justification for; justify: *Ignorance of the law excuses no one.*

4. to release from an obligation or duty: *to be excused from jury duty.*

5. to seek or obtain exemption or release for (oneself): *to excuse oneself from a meeting*

Notice what excuses are your favorites. *Not enough time. Too busy. Forgot. Had to help someone.* They may all be true, but they are still excuses.

When you have an accountability partner (see goal session), he or she will help you explore your excuses. We are all given twenty-four hours in a day. How we use them is up to us. Is your vision not powerful enough to have you let go of what will not move you forward in favor of putting in a new behavior that will assure your success? Are your goals unrealistic considering all of your musts? Revise them. Always keep your word to yourself or you will teach yourself not to trust. Did you abandon your goal this week to help someone in need? Once or twice we may put aside what we are working on, but when we continually give up ourselves in favor of another, we are saying there is no power. There is no power for our loved one to call on for assistance, and there is no power we are able to master to assure we will accomplish what we received in our vision. What old belief, old behavior, old thought can you release to move to your next level of growth?

What old grudge are you still hanging on to that blocks you from your joy? There is an excellent saying that when we refuse to forgive it is like drinking poison and expecting the person to die. Forgiveness is not for the person who wounded you. Forgiveness is for you. If you find that you cannot or will not release a long-held grudge, get help in letting it go. There are excellent coaches, therapists, and books that help in the forgiveness process. Take advantage of what is available to you.

Exercise Session 7

1. Begin to be aware of what your excuses are. Write them on 3 x 5 cards and keep them close to you. Once you have gone two weeks not using a particular excuse, you may burn or throw your excuse away. You may also pass it on to someone who needs a good excuse.

2. Make a list of all those people, situations, and events that you could forgive. Notice what you want to forgive and what you would still hold onto. Ask yourself what you get from holding the grudge.

3. Clean out your home of all that is not a part of who you are today. Box up what you may want to look at again in the future, donate what you know will never serve you, and throw out what will serve no one. Celebrate your release!

TIERS OF HEALING III
SESSION 8
BOUNDARIES

*Children need **boundaries** and ground rules.*
When children don`t have structure, they make up their own rules and
negative behavior is what they use to get your attention.
—Jo Frost

Song: "Keep Your Hands to Yourself" by Georgia Satellites

The best explanation of boundaries and boundary setting is the following story.

Imagine you own a good size ranch with enough grass and water to feed and care for the cattle you own. You have no fences and trust that there is enough for all in the area.

Your neighbor begins to herd some of his cattle onto your land. At first you tell yourself that he must have a good reason for allowing so many of his cattle to graze on your land and trust he will rectify the situation. The following month your foreman tells you again of the neighbor's cattle grazing on your land. You now have a cup of coffee with your neighbor and ask that he please corral his herd and inform him that your foreman has noticed an increase of cattle not belonging to you on your land. Your neighbor apologizes and assures you no harm was done, and you part friends assuming he will take care of the problem. You do not like confrontation and say a silent prayer that your neighbor is still friendly.

The following month you begin to notice a huge increase of cattle at your watering hole. Sure enough they are your neighbor's cattle. You go to his home immediately and inform him that his cattle must remain on his land. This time your neighbor tells you his watering hole is drying up, and it will cost him money to locate a new watering area. He thought you were a good neighbor but perhaps you are not. You tell him you are sorry but at the rate of use you will soon be out of water yourself and need to dig another watering hole. Your neighbor smiles and says, "Right." You are sure he understands.

Of course his cattle continue to graze your land and drink your water. You decide to put up a fence. Your neighbor now comes over storming, yelling, and calling you names. He sees you as stingy, greedy, and unfriendly and tells you, you will be responsible for the death of his cattle.

What do you do?

Depending on your answer, you will be able to see how you set boundaries. The majority of people I have worked with over several years do not set boundaries for themselves or others. Inner boundaries and a sense of self-discipline to accomplish your goals and visions cannot be actualized if you have no outer boundaries. I believe this lack of boundaries is what truly trips people as they attempt to move forward and achieve success.

Those individuals brave enough to begin to make boundaries for their children, spouses, ex-spouses, and family expect that their family will gladly embrace the new set of rules and life will be filled with smiles. This is not the case.

People want to do what they want to do when they want to do it. They do not want you or anyone telling them they must now change. In addition to setting a boundary, it is necessary to have a consequence for ignoring the boundary. Remember our ranchers? If the fence gets knocked down, the sheriff must be called and the fence repaired. If not, there was no reason to build the fence, and the time and money were wasted.

A word of caution, be certain that whatever consequence you come up with you will be willing to enforce. Do not teach people and yourself that your word holds no power.

What power have you given away? Begin to take it back by writing down what boundaries you have and what the result of ignoring them is. Do this for those around you and also for yourself. For example, perhaps you have given your power to make healthy food choices away to your partner. You have asked that he buys and prepares healthier food items and does not offer you high-calorie, high-fat, and high-sugar goodies in the evening. You must first start by writing down what your boundary is (ex.: No sugar, no white flour) and what you will do if presented with this type of food (If N. asks me if I want a donut, I will say no and then leave the room and go to a different part of the house, and if need be I will throw the package of donuts in the trash the next day). It is now up to you to enforce this boundary. Expect N to be upset and for N to tell you he has the right to eat what he wants. He may eat whatever he wants, and you have the right to remove yourself from the foods that trigger you and to throw them away if they are left for the next day. This will cause a confrontation. You will live through a confrontation, and eventually N will either stop offering you donuts or he will eat them somewhere else.

Exercise Session 8

1. Identify three areas of your life where you allow others to take away your power and choice. Begin slowly to set up boundaries to take back your power. This does not need to involve anger. Good boundaries are set in an atmosphere of calm and delivered with assurance.

2. Set one internal boundary for yourself and decide what the consequence will be if you break your word. Share this with your accountability partner.

TIERS OF HEALING III
SESSION 9
PICTURE IT™

The main theme to emerge...is that there appear to be two modes of thinking, verbal and nonverbal, represented rather separately in left and right hemispheres respectively and that our education system, as well as science in general, tends to neglect the nonverbal form of intellect. What it comes down to is that modern society discriminates against the right hemisphere.
—Roger Sperry (1973)

Song: "Every Picture Tells a Story" by Ronald David Wood/Steve Harley

In 1981 Roger Sperry received the Nobel Prize for his discoveries concerning the differences between the right and left hemispheres of our brains. This information has made it possible for us to create effective ways to solve problems, envision solutions, and visualize success.

The basics concerning Sperry's work show that our cerebral cortex has a left and a right hemisphere and while the right hemisphere is active the left hemisphere is at rest. Each hemisphere has specific tasks and skills. Our schools educate the left hemisphere of our brains, and those same schools ignore the powerful right hemisphere.

Picture It™, created by Anne Browning, is a tool that uses the power of the right brain to set goals, create visions, and solve problems by utilizing the powerful way in which our brains work.

The right hemisphere of the brain thinks in symbols, pictures, patterns, and the left hemisphere uses words. It is more complicated than what is written here, and there is new information and discoveries every year. For more information, Google Sperry or Right/Left Brain Hemispheres.

As you now have made your way to a place where you notice the power of your thoughts and the use of intent to laser that intent into success, you may be experiencing obstacles or boulders in your way. Despite setting boundaries and having a powerful vision and specific goals, you may still find yourself not achieving what you desire.

You may find yourself saying words such as, "I feel as if I am stuck in mud" or "It feels as if I am on a cliff and there is no way down." "It feels as if there is a brick wall between me and what I want."

All of the words describe a type of picture, which is how the right hemisphere sees problems. The right hemisphere creates an inner picture, and then our left brain uses words, logic, and numbers to solve the problem. The left brain attempts to analyze and solve the issue, but the picture in the right hemisphere remains.

Let's look at an example. Mary has a vision of returning to school to obtain her nursing degree so she can support herself and her two daughters after a messy divorce. She has a great vision board, which she looks at daily, and she has specific achievable goals that she has written down on her calendar. She has set up clear, written boundaries to allow herself time to study. Despite all her work, Mary is still unable to calm her nerves when she takes exams.

Working with her accountability partner, Mary shares that she feels as if she is facing the monster from under the bed every time she takes a test. Mary knows she has test anxiety; she had it years ago in college. She thought if she studied more and set up quiz times to do sample tests, it would help her feel more confident, and she would not only feel less shaky when testing but would also do better on her exams. This has not happened, and on nights that Mary knows she will have a test in the morning, she cannot sleep.

Her partner has her draw the feeling she shared, the "as if" feeling. Mary draws a small girl shaking in bed and a huge hairy hand coming out from under the bed getting ready to grab the little girl. The picture is all purples, blacks, and reds.

Once Mary has her drawing, her accountability partner asks her, "What would you add to this picture to have the little girl feel safe?" Mary laughs and says, "I would scratch out the monster." That is not how our brains work; we cannot just scratch things out, but we can add something. Mary thinks and eventually adds a wand that she draws in the girl's hand. The wand has the words, "Monster Evaporator." As Mary draws this, she can feel herself breathe more deeply, and she feels something lift. Two weeks later she receives an A on her exam, and her test anxiety has lessened.

Picture It™ has been used with hundreds of people, and all report significant change in their problem(s). This is a simple, effective tool with which to alter your inner pictures.

Steps for Picture It™

1. Define how you feel using the "as if" model. (ex.: I feel as if I have a dog chasing me; I feel as if I am underwater; I feel as if I am going in circles; I feel as if I am all alone and no one can help; etc.)

2. Draw this feeling in crayon on white paper.

3. Allow yourself to look at the picture as if it was a person in a play or movie or somehow separate from you. Imagine that this person in your picture really is underwater or being chased by a dog, whatever. Using your imagination, ask yourself, "What would I add to this scene to help this person?" Remember, you cannot take anything away—you can only add something to the picture.

4. Now draw what needs to be added to help the person. Be certain it is something you could actually imagine doing.

5. Once you draw the solution, keep it close to you and allow the solution to enter the right side of your brain. Keep the new picture in your awareness.

6. Please report your results to anne@tiersofhealing.com.

Exercise Session 9

Do the above steps and let us know the results.

Exercise Session 9

TIERS OF HEALING III
SESSION 10
LIFE AT ITS BEST

I do not think that the measure of a civilization is how tall its buildings of concrete are,
but rather how well its people have learned to relate to their environment and fellow man.
Sun Bear of the Chippewa

Song: "Open Up Your Heart and Let the Sunshine In" Frente

Wow! You have made it to the end of these sessions. Congratulations on your courage, perseverance, and willingness.

Who can you share your success with? Who will help you celebrate? It is important to celebrate yourself and share your success with others. Give voice to the journey you have been on. Give voice to your new reality.

Tiers of Healing has groups that gather to explore many of the sessions presented in this self-study guide. Once we reach the last session, we celebrate. We have worked hard, confronted our fears, and moved closer to a vision that will help us reach our new normal. We deserve fun.

What is your idea of life at its best? Is it a beach hideaway or jet setting from five-star hotel to five-star hotel? Perhaps life at its best is just getting through each day with a smile on your face. Have you put all that you love on your vision board, and have you allowed for fun, for play?

Fun and play are vital parts of the human experience and are necessary for a full life. When was the last time you played? Google and other companies are realizing the importance of play to increase productivity and have set up areas in the company for their employees to play. Swimming pools, exercise areas, games, and silly items all relieve the intensity of every day and increase creativity as it increases the bottom line for Google.

The left hemisphere of the brain begins to decrease in effectiveness after about one and half hours. The right side of the brain actually increases our energy while we utilize it. The right side of the brain is in charge of such things as rhythm, senses, big-picture items, intuition, and connection. These things are all involved in fun. Laughing has been shown to provide some of the same endorphins as long-distance running without the sweat. There are even Laughing Clubs that meet daily and weekly to laugh.

The use of laughter and humor has been documented in the healing process. Norman Cousins, in his 1979 book *Anatomy of an Illness*, describes how watching funny movies actually helped him recover. Start laughing.

In addition to laughing and playing, gratitude will open your door to joy. It is always possible to find one thing daily to be grateful for. A gratitude journal or diary will help you track all the good in your life. Once you begin to see the good, you begin to expect the good. It is all win-win.

Life at its best must include time spent outside. So many of us go from house to garage to car to underground garage to office and then back again. We rarely spend time listening to birds or smelling flowers. Even our children are not getting enough of the sunshine vitamin (vitamin D) as they are shuttled from school to play dates and video games. Nature has the ability to nurture us and feed our souls.

Laughter, play, nature, and gratitude all combine to provide us a life at its best.

Exercise Session 10

The exercise is to have fun. You have earned it. Go play.

You have now completed *Tier III: Journey To A New Vision.* As your life lengthens, you will continue to add additional visions, and what you have learned and experienced in these ten sessions will serve you and enhance your life.

Remember to keep your vision ever present and allow those feelings to draw you forward. If you stumble in completing your goals, start again. Life is all about showing up, and as long as you keep focusing and refocusing, you will get to where you want to be.

If at any time you get stuck or have questions, please remember we are here to serve you. Our wish is that the paths we have forged will be walked on by multitudes. If this guide has helped you, we would like to know. We would appreciate you passing on our site and letting others know there is a place of hope.

May your life be all it can be,
Anne

www.ingramcontent.com/pod-product-compliance
Lightning Source LLC
Chambersburg PA
CBHW081528040426
42447CB00013B/3372